HOW TO LEAD WITH GENIUS

Words of Wisdom for the Common Sense Manager

HOW TO LEAD WITH GENIUS

Words of Wisdom for the Common Sense Manager

Walter P. von Wartburg

MARKUS WIENER PUBLISHING, INC.,
AND
SHAPOLSKY PUBLISHERS, INC.,
NEW YORK

A Shapolsky Book

For additional information, contact:
Shapolsky Publishers, Inc.
136 West 22nd Street, New York, NY 10011
(212) 633-2022; FAX (212) 633-2123
and
Markus Wiener Publishing Inc.,
225 Lafayette Street, Suite 911, New York, NY 10012
(212) 941-1324 and (212) 947-6100

10 9 8 7 6 5 4 3 2 1

Library of Congress Cataloging-in-Publication Data:

Wartburg, Walter P. von, 19–
How to lead with genius : words of wisdom for the common sense
manager / by Walter P. von Wartburg.
p.   cm.
ISBN 0-945179-02-2
1. Industrial management—decision making. 2. Leadership.
I. Title.
HD30.23.W37   1991
658.4'092—dc20   90-8141

Typography by Smith, Inc., New York, NY
Manufactured in the United States of America

Common sense
is not so common.

— Voltaire

CONTENTS

2 — *If you take people the way they are, you are not likely to get better ones*

3 — *No industry is so mature that it no longer needs to innovate*

4 — *Choose good experts, not friendly ones*

5 — *Lawyers are meant to help you run the business, not to run the business*

6 — *Control the planners, otherwise they may control you*

7 — *The invention of Lotus 1-2-3 should not substitute sensitivity analysis for sound reasoning and judgment*

8 — *Bureaucracy is the only real threat to both* glasnost *and entrepreneurship*

9 — *The dinosaurs may have died out because they grew too heavy to search for food; fat organizations risk the same fate*

10 — *Quality, like productivity, can be improved only by people; give them the right incentives*

Chapter 5
COMMON SENSE IN MANAGING THE
OUTSIDE WORLD: 91

THE MAIN OUTSIGHTS

1 — *An organization performs best if it satisfies the needs of markets and customers*

2 — *Competition works, either for you or against you*

3 — *Public opinion is an important element of success or failure in business*

4 — *Industry is part of society; society is part of politics; therefore, politics always sets the context for any business*

5 — *As long as people read newspapers and watch television, the media will play a decisive role in every facet of business*

6 — *Moving means progressing; nobody achieves anything by standing still*

7 — *Respect the law, but don't always follow the advice of lawyers*

8 — *A good conscience is the best memory*

9 — *The acid test of ethical standards is their implementation*

PREFACE

This publication is about common sense in leadership. It contains some of the main ingredients of common sense leadership, describes the important characteristics and lists the tasks of leading with common sense. It also provides some essential insights and "outsights" for managing an organization and its environment.

The book consists of quotations from outstanding individuals who have enriched humankind with their wisdom over the centuries. The mere survival of these quotations, and of the works they come from, is living proof of the inner value they still contain today. They express a tradition to be cherished.

The quotes are complemented by what I consider sound common sense advice, based on twenty-five years of management experience in small and large organizations of government, academia and business. They are meant to provide some guidelines for what we all believe we are — or want to become — namely, Common Sense Leaders.

The combination of quotes and advice is intended to stimulate you to remember situations in which you acted against common sense. Everybody carries a personal museum of such memories in his or her head, which should come to life as you read *How to Lead with Genius: Words of Wisdom for the Common Sense Manager.* Reliving past events and looking differently at present problems may bring common sense into focus, and enable you to use it consistently, now and in the future.

Walter P. von Wartburg
Basel and New York
1991

INTRODUCTION:
THE UNCOMMON ORIGINS OF COMMON SENSE

The concept of "common sense" has always been dear to Americans. Yankee ingenuity, frontier resourcefulness and Midwestern practicality are clichés of American character. Indeed, the United States might never have existed were it not for Tom Paine's revolutionary pamphlet *Common Sense.* Published in 1776, this booklet brought the rising Revolutionary sentiment into sharp focus by placing the blame for the suffering of the colonies directly on the reigning British monarch, George III. Paine argued that instead of merely protesting British taxation policies, the colonies should incorporate in their goals a demand for independence. The 50-page pamphlet sold more than half a million copies in the space of a few months and paved the way for the Declaration of Independence on July 4.

The notion of common sense was already familiar in philosophy; it is mentioned in the work of Aristotle and Epictetus. At about the same time in history as Paine was writing, the Scottish philosopher Thomas Reid was devising his "common sense philosophy." It held that in the actual perceptions of unsophisticated men, sensations are not mere ideas or subjective impressions, but carry with them basic beliefs. Such beliefs, he insisted, belong to the common sense and reason of mankind. In matters of common sense, he felt that "the learned and the unlearned, the philosopher and the day laborer, are upon one and the same level."

Some one hundred years later, the British philosopher George Edward Moore was once again preoccupied with common sense problems, such as the nature of perception as it relates to material things. He became the founding father of analytic philosophy in, among other works, his "Defense of Common Sense," published in 1923.

Since then, the notion of Common Sense has crept into all facets of modern life. Common sense approaches are used for the description of holistic models of health and disease; they are found in scientific approaches for dealing with uncertainty; and they form parts of expert systems for artificial intelligence and computer programming.

Common sense is less prevalent in the management literature, though one finds topical interest in common sense in personal management treatises. Some common sense advice is also available for a variety of specific activities, ranging from cost-saving mechanics to improving logistics. However, there is a crying need for a more comprehensive approach. In a world where specialized knowledge and expertise are at a premium, a "back to common sense" approach would be particularly welcome in the teaching of management sciences. Graduates of MBA schools more often than not are simply "confused at a higher level" when they enter real business life. They have been taught all the intricacies of modern management techniques. What they need to learn on the job and in their personal life-styles is the application of basic common sense to complex situations.

This book attempts to counterbalance the heavy baggage of specialized knowledge and expertise with some good common sense advice and experience. In its attempt to do so, constant reference is made to past genius. Commonsensical quotations outlive the personalities to whom they are attributed. Their truth and wisdom assure them eternal life. They may guide us in our day-to-day search for practical solutions to increasingly complex problems.

Such was the uncommon origin of the common sense words of wisdom, here compiled for good use by today's executives.

Chapter 1
COMMON SENSE MANAGEMENT: THE MAIN INGREDIENTS

• • • • • • • • •

To judge from the increasingly specialized management literature one might conclude that management has become a science of expert systems, special techniques and sophisticated computer skills. These tools may, indeed, be helpful in many cases. A need exists, however, also to bring basic common sense back into focus. Leadership is an art mastered most successfully by individuals who rely on established principles of common sense.

Common sense is not always easy to identify. These simple but profound principles have different expressions in different situations. The manifestations of common sense in a European country or in a small organization may vary from those in the United States or in a large institution. Nevertheless, its underlying foundations have endured and been recognized as valuable over centuries. In today's technical world common sense is again much in demand, and for good reason.

The term *management* is equally ill-defined. To some it means getting things done by others. To many it represents a sometimes cumbersome way of earning a living. And to a few, it evokes associations of leadership, moving ahead, setting the pace and becoming successful.

The goal is to combine "Common Sense" and "Leadership" in order to achieve Common Sense Leadership reflected in the following main ingredients:

- holding to convictions, while tolerating ambiguity
- sustaining leadership and making decisions
- confronting risks and accepting criticism
- relishing change, while relying on experience
- accepting perceptions as reality and making effective use of one's own perceived personality

3

INGREDIENT 1

To be convinced of what one wants to achieve

Holding to Convictions...

The reasonable man adapts himself to the world; the unreasonable one persists in trying to adapt the world to himself. Therefore, all progress depends on the unreasonable man.
— George Bernard Shaw (1856–1950)

One man with courage is a majority.
—Thomas Jefferson (1743–1826)

Any coward can fight a battle when he's sure of winning.
— George Eliot (1819–1880)

It is better to be envied than pitied.
— Herodotus (c. 485–425 B.C.)

Nothing is more conducive to peace of mind than not having any opinion at all.
— Georg Christoph Lichtenberg (1742–1799)

It is easy to have principles when you are rich. The important thing is to have principles when you are poor.
— Ray A. Kroc (1902–1984)

Reason and judgment are the qualities of a leader.
— Cornelius Tacitus (c. 55–c. 117 A.D.)

The Common Sense Manager

- holds to a clear set of convictions, beliefs and value judgments
- knows that convictions carry a lot of power
- never forgets, however, that it is sometimes easier to subscribe to principles than to live up to them
- takes a firm stand on basic values and fundamental principles as essential elements for success
- sees the need of human beings for association with specific belief systems and principles
- explains his convictions, thereby linking meaningful values to individual jobs and activities

INGREDIENT 2

To overcome ambiguity and still get there

. . .While Tolerating Ambiguity

Life is the art of drawing sufficient conclusions from
insufficient premises.
— Samuel Butler (1835–1902)

The test of a first-rate intelligence is the ability to hold two
opposed ideas in the mind at the same time, and still retain
the ability to function.
— F. Scott Fitzgerald (1896–1940)

All business proceeds on beliefs, on judgments of probabilities, and not on certainties.
— Charles W. Eliot (1834–1926)

When nothing is sure, everything is possible.
— Margaret Drabble (1939–)

A reasonable probability is the only certainty.
— Edgar Watson Howe (1853–1937)

The well-bred contradict other people. The wise contradict
themselves.
— Oscar Wilde (1854–1900)

The Common Sense Manager

- knows that tolerance of ambiguity distinguishes the more
  intelligent from the less intelligent executive
- understands that managing ambiguity is a constant
  learning process
- does not shy away from deciding "yes" or "no" on the
  basis of contradictory data
- realizes that conflicting signals may be good for testing the
  tolerance-of-ambiguity level of senior people, but that they
  are confusing for operational management
- tries, therefore, to accomplish goal congruence by aligning
  individual goals with company objectives

INGREDIENT 3

To accept loneliness and never give up

Sustaining Leadership. . .

The strongest man in the world is he who stands most alone.
—Henrik Ibsen (1828–1906)

You see, that's what fame is: solitude.
—Coco Chanel (1883–1971)

To be a leader of men one must turn one's back on men.
—Havelock Ellis (1859–1939)

It is personalities, not principles, that move the age.
—Oscar Wilde (1854–1900)

When the best leader's work is done, the people say,
"We did it ourselves."
—Lao-tzu (c. 604–c. 531 B.C.)

The Common Sense Manager

- comprehends leadership as agenda-setting, decision-making and delineation of concepts for implementation
- values his personal sensibility more than any technical sensitivity analysis
- knows how to turn uncertainty into risk
- establishes personal relationships
- is able to instill individuals at all levels with a sense of initiative and responsibility
- accepts responsibility and is willing to be held accountable
- practices leadership as the art of letting others have their way

INGREDIENT 4

To make decisions despite uncertainty

. . .and Making Decisions

At twenty the will rules; at thirty the intellect; at forty the judgment.
— *Baltasar Gracián (1601–1658)*

Nothing is more difficult, and therefore more precious, than to be able to decide.
— *Napoleon Bonaparte (1769–1821)*

He that forecasts all difficulties that he may meet with in business, will never set about it.
— *James Kelly (n.d./18th century)*

Every step forward is made at the cost of mental and physical pain to someone.
— *Friedrich Wilhelm Nietzsche (1844–1900)*

The task of management is not to apply a formula but to decide issues on a case-by-case basis.
— *Alfred P. Sloan, Jr. (1875–1966)*

As for accomplishments, I just did what I had to do as things came along.
— *Eleanor Roosevelt (1884–1962)*

The Common Sense Manager

- translates uncertainties into risks, so that he can decide
- believes in his capacity to decide and set priorities
- knows that a quick "no" at the beginning hurts less than an initial "maybe" and a "no" at the end
- provokes and listens to differing opinions, but makes his own decisions
- makes decisions consistent with his vision, strategy goals and objectives
- postpones the final decision on an important issue by one week, if unanimous agreement was reached too fast

INGREDIENT 5

To see risk-taking as a natural prerequisite for success

Confronting Risks...

Boldness in business is the first, second, and third thing.
—Thomas Fuller (1654–1734)

Not failure, but low aim, is crime.
—James Russell Lowell (1819–1891)

Take calculated risks. That is quite different from being rash.
—George S. Patton (1885–1945)

Any man can make mistakes, but only an idiot persists in his error.
—Marcus Tullius Cicero (106–43 B.C.)

It is hard to look up to a leader who keeps his ear to the ground.
—James H. Boren (1925–)

Everybody knows if you are too careful you are so occupied in being careful that you are sure to stumble over something.
—Gertrude Stein (1874–1946)

The Athenians are capable both of taking risks and estimating them beforehand.
—Thucydides (c. 460–400 B.C.),
quoting Pericles (c. 495–429 B.C.)

The Common Sense Manager

- is a risk-taker by nature

- sees risk as a necessary element in human evolution

- encourages risk-taking by means of adequate reward systems

- learns from the failures of others instead of criticizing them

- knows that confronting risks is a prerequisite for getting benefits

INGREDIENT 6

To accept and evaluate criticism

. . .and Accepting Criticism

I know that they are most deceived that trusteth most in themselves.
— *Elizabeth I (1533–1603)*

Man errs as long as he strives.
— *Johann Wolfgang von Goethe (1749–1832)*

Failure is instructive. The person who really thinks, learns quite as much from his failures as from his successes.
— *John Dewey (1859–1952)*

To escape criticism—do nothing, say nothing, be nothing.
— *Elbert Hubbard (1856–1915)*

As far as criticism is concerned, we don't resent that, unless it is absolutely biased, as it is in most cases.
— *John Vorster (1915–1983)*

It is criticism that the future belongs to.
— *Oscar Wilde (1854–1900)*

The Common Sense Manager

- accepts criticism as a way of finding out how others perceive reality
- admits mistakes, so he can learn from them
- realizes that bad excuses are worse than none
- does not defend the faults of the past, but uses them to impact positively on the quality of decisions about the future
- speaks out truthfully, even when it hurts

INGREDIENT 7

*To see change as painful in the short term, lack of
change as destructive in the long term*

Relishing Change...

All is change; all yields its place and goes.
—Euripides (480–405 B.C.)

Nothing is permanent but change. *—Heraclitus (c. 535–475 B.C.)*

The law must be stable, but it must not stand still.
—Roscoe Pound (1870–1964)

New opinions are always suspected, and usually opposed, without any other reason, but because they are not already common.
—John Locke (1632–1704)

In the world there are only two tragedies: One is not getting what one wants, and the other is getting it.
—Oscar Wilde (1854–1900)

The Common Sense Manager

- strives to master change and monitors continuity

- creates useful change where feasible, avoids change that is not useful—and distinguishes between the two

- understands the basic framework and political process in which change takes place

- knows that innovation is taking place when everybody opposes an idea

- does not change a strategy if it works

INGREDIENT 8

To learn from experience, good or bad

. . .While Relying on Experience

Experience is the name everyone gives to their mistakes.
—Oscar Wilde (1854–1900)

The things which hurt, instruct.
—Benjamin Franklin (1706–1790)

Life can only be understood backwards, but it must be lived
forwards.
—Søren Kierkegaard (1813–1855)

There is the greatest practical benefit in making a few
failures early in life.
—Thomas Henry Huxley (1825–1895)

The wider the experience, the stronger the personality.
—Indira Gandhi (1917–1987)

If at first you don't succeed, try, try again. Then quit. There's
no sense being a damn fool about it.
—W. C. Fields (1880–1946)

The Common Sense Manager

- integrates experience into action

- works hard to steepen his experience curve

- knows that personal experience is difficult to transmit to
  others

- values personal experience as much as theoretical
  modeling

- relies for qualitative judgments on his experience rather
  than on statistical expertise

INGREDIENT 9

To give importance to perception

Accepting Perceptions as Reality. . .

Beauty is altogether in the eye of the beholder.
— Lew Wallace (1827–1905)

To his dog, every man is Napoleon; hence the constant popularity of dogs.
—Aldous Leonard Huxley (1894–1963)

To be a great champion you must believe that you're the best. If you're not, pretend you are.
—Muhammad Ali (1942–)

People only see what they are prepared to see.
— Ralph Waldo Emerson (1803–1882)

What the multitude says, is so, or soon will be so.
— Baltasar Gracián (1601–1658)

Our government rests on public opinion. Whoever can change public opinion, can change the government.
—Abraham Lincoln (1809–1865)

The Common Sense Manager

- knows that as shares of market are important for the product, shares of mind are essential for the company

- perceives public opinion as being often more telling than published opinion

- deals differently with reality and perceived reality

- keeps an open window to the outside world and respects differing perceptions

INGREDIENT 10

*To put the perception of one's own
personality to work*

. . .and Making Effective Use of One's Own Perceived Personality

There are times when the belief of the people, though it may be without ground, is as significant as the truth.
— Friedrich von Schiller (1759–1805)

It is only shallow people who do not judge by appearances.
— Oscar Wilde (1854–1900)

The greatest deception men suffer is from their own opinions.
— Leonardo da Vinci (1452–1519)

The man is only half himself, the other half is his expression.
— Ralph Waldo Emerson (1803–1882)

In order to be irreplaceable one must always be different.
— Margaret Sanger (1883–1966)

He who knows others is learned; he who knows himself is wise.
— Lao-tzu (c. 604–c. 531 B.C.)

The Common Sense Leader

- knows that symbols are important and makes effective use of them
- realizes that he achieves more with perceptions about him than with his actual presence
- asks trusted people for his perceived phantom picture
- tries to change perceptions by changing style and personal behavior—and *vice versa*
- builds up a record of reliability and predictability

SUMMING UP

Common sense is as rare as genius.

— Ralph Waldo Emerson (1803–1882)

Chapter 2

THE COMMON SENSE MANAGER: THE MAIN CHARACTERISTICS

• • • • • • • • •

The Common Sense Manager—whether a man or a woman—has a number of *characteristics* which distinguish him or her from the average high-tech, low-touch executive. Those characteristics are not so very special. They are commonsensical. It may be this commonsensical nature which makes them so rare in the world of managers.

There is a commonplace image of today's manager. He or she is driven by outside events, loses control over his or her agenda, is power-hungry, manipulates people, is a workaholic without sufficient time for friends and family, and accumulates risk factors to health, waking up in a hospital bed after a frenzied life of decision-making, often too late.

Not so the Common Sense Manager. He or she:

- is a personality perfecter
- accepts power as a responsibility
- invests in people
- relies on heart and head
- respects both work and leisure
- practices a healthy lifestyle
- is in control of personal risk factors
- builds lasting friendships
- accepts happiness
- values common sense as a guiding principle

CHARACTERISTIC 1

"Personality Perfector"—The difference between a person and a personality lies in the amount of work by the former on the latter

Perfecting the Personality

A man's character is his fate.

—Heraclitus (c. 535–c. 475 B.C.)

Character is made by what you stand for; reputation, by what you fall for.

—Robert Quillen (1887–1948)

Our deeds determine us, as much as we determine our deeds.

—George Eliot (1819–1880)

Few people do business well who do nothing else.

—Philip Dormer Stanhope, Earl of Chesterfield (1694–1773)

You are, when all is done—just what you are.

—Johann Wolfgang von Goethe (1749–1832)

Those who do not complain are never pitied.

—Jane Austen (1775–1817)

He is not laughed at that laughs at himself first.

—Thomas Fuller (1654–1734)

The Common Sense Manager

- knows that personality is composed of character and conduct
- changes at least his conduct, if he cannot improve on his character
- is able to distinguish right from wrong and good from bad
- tries to be tolerant
- seeks out harmony in discord
- aspires to increase control over life events

CHARACTERISTIC 2

*"Realizes power equals responsibility"—The more power
one achieves, the more responsibility one assumes.
And vice versa*

Accepting Power as a Responsibility

Power tends to corrupt, and absolute power corrupts
absolutely.
—Lord John Emerich Edward Acton (1834–1902)

The measure of man is what he does with power.
—Pittacus (c. 650–c. 570 B.C.)

What lies in our power to do, lies in our power not to do.
—Aristotle (384–322 B.C.)

All executive power—from the reign of ancient kings to the rule
of modern dictators—has the outward appearance of efficiency.
—William O. Douglas (1898–1980)

The megalomaniac differs from the narcissist by the fact that
he wishes to be powerful rather than charming, and seeks
to be feared rather than loved. To this type belong many
lunatics and most of the great men of history.
—Bertrand Russell (1872–1970)

Power and violence are opposites; where the one rules
absolutely, the other is absent.
—Hannah Arendt (1906–1975)

RHIP/RHIR Rank has its privileges, rank has its responsibilities.
—U.S. Army expression taught to all commissioned officers

The Common Sense Manager

- enjoys power because it increases his ability to obtain
  desired results
- uses power skillfully as the capacity to ensure the outcomes
  he wishes
- builds checks and balances into his power system to limit
  abuses, including his own
- sees no contradiction between individual power and social
  responsibility
- realizes that the exercise of power is best based on
  exchange that satisfies mutual needs

CHARACTERISTIC 3

"People-mindedness"—People matter. So do products, profitability and progress. But people matter more

Investing in People

By nature, men are nearly alike; by practice, they get to be widely different.
— Confucius (c. 551–c. 479 B.C.)

Though all men be made of one metal, yet they be not cast all in one mold.
— John Lyly (1554–1606)

Selfishness must always be forgiven, you know, because there is no hope of a cure.
— Jane Austen (1775–1817)

I don't want any yes-men around me. I want everybody to tell me the truth even if it costs them their jobs.
— Samuel Goldwyn (1882–1974)

Conservatives are not necessarily stupid, but most stupid people are conservatives.
— John Stuart Mill (1806–1873)

Human nature is the same everywhere; the modes only are different.
— Philip Dormer Stanhope, Earl of Chesterfield (1694–1773)

The old believe everything, the middle-aged suspect everything, the young know everything.
— Oscar Wilde (1854–1900)

Macho does not prove mucho.
— Zsa Zsa Gabor (1919–)

The Common Sense Manager

- has the capacity to motivate, to win and to retain trust
- is people-oriented
- does not display in the treatment of his inferiors what he dislikes in his superiors
- knows that fear of failure is a more powerful incentive than eagerness to succeed
- realizes that the size of a problem can be determined only by the person who is facing it
- realizes that inertia is the common thread of collective action, corporate or communal

CHARACTERISTIC 4

*"Lack of tunnel vision"—Relies on two brains—
left and right—one heart and a lot of instincts, as the
ingredients of sound judgment*

Relying On Heart and Head

We distrust our heart too much, and our head not enough.
—Joseph Roux (1834–1905)

It is the heart always that sees, before the head can see.
—Thomas Carlyle (1795–1881)

It is only with the heart that one can see rightly; what is essential is invisible to the eye.
—Antoine de Saint-Exupéry (1900–1944)

The heart of a fool is in his mouth, but the mouth of a wise man is in his heart.
—Benjamin Franklin (1706–1790)

If you are not a liberal at age 20, you have no heart; if you are not a conservative at age 40, you have no brain.
—Winston L. S. Churchill (1874–1965)

The way to the head leads through the heart.
—Friedrich von Schiller (1759–1805)

The Common Sense Manager

- has a clear set of personal priorities and values
- combines rationality and efficiency with emotionality and patience
- accepts that values are as diverse and different as individuals themselves
- relies on his heart at least as often as he relies on his logic
- knows that at the end of the day his work is going to be judged in a framework of values, not just on the basis of numbers

CHARACTERISTIC 5

"On/Off Personality" — Works hard and enjoys hard, never attempts one without the other

Respecting Both Work and Leisure

To the art of working well a civilized race would add the art of playing well.
— *George Santayana (1863–1952)*

Most men that do thrive in the world do forget to take pleasure during the time that they are getting their estate, but reserve that till they have got one, and then it is too late for them to enjoy it.
— *Samuel Pepys (1633–1703)*

There are two things to aim at in life: first, to get what you want; and, after that, to enjoy it. Only the wisest of mankind achieve the second.
— *Logan Pearsall Smith (1865–1946)*

He that will make a good use of any part of his life must allow a large part of it to recreation.
— *John Locke (1632–1704)*

Leisure for men of business, and business for men of leisure, would cure many companies.
— *Hester Lynch Thrale Piozzi (1741–1821)*

The goal of war is peace; of business, leisure.
— *Aristotle (384–322 B.C.)*

It is in our idleness, our dreams, that the submerged truth sometimes comes to the top.
— *Virginia Woolf (1882–1941)*

The Common Sense Manager

- knows that the busiest people have the most leisure
- knows that graveyards are full of irreplaceable people
- does not overreact to minor issues
- retains a healthy distance from even the biggest problems
- maintains and enjoys an optimal level of chaos
- foregoes business travel during important birthdays, anniversaries and other social events
- values his family at least as much as his work
- plans vacations well ahead and takes them

CHARACTERISTIC 6

"Health-Consciousness"—Invests in health to provide a return which can be measured in added quality of life

Practicing a Healthy Lifestyle

The health of the people is really the foundation upon which all their happiness and all their powers as a state depend.
— Benjamin Disraeli, Earl of Beaconsfield (1804–1881)

To rise at six, to dine at ten, to sup at six, to sleep at ten, makes a man live for ten times ten.
—Victor Hugo (1802–1885)

Never work before breakfast; if you have to work before breakfast, get your breakfast first.
— Josh Billings (1818–1885)

Our aches and pains conform to opinion. A man is as miserable as he thinks he is.
— Lucius Annaeus Seneca (c. 4 B.C.–65 A.D.)

Love never dies of starvation, but often of indigestion.
— Ninon de Lenclos (1620–1705)

Most men spend the first half of their lives making the second half miserable.
— Jean de La Bruyère (1645–1696)

Preserving the health by too severe a rule is a wearisome malady.
— François, Duc de La Rochefoucauld (1613–1680)

The Common Sense Manager

- knows that his good health is his biggest asset

- sees life as too short to worry about minor issues

- invests in his health as he does in his business — i.e., with a long-term view to Return on Investment (ROI)

- cherishes physical vitality and good stamina as essential attributes of success

- is health conscious, but prefers adding life to years rather than years to life

CHARACTERISTIC 7

*"In control of body and soul" — The survival of the fittest
needs practice in the gym, in the bookstore
and at the table*

Controlling Personal Risk Factors

By too much sitting still the body becomes unhealthy; and soon the mind.
—*Henry Wadsworth Longfellow (1807–1882)*

Bodily exercises are to be done discreetly; not to be taken evenly and alike by all men.
—*Thomas à Kempis (1380–1447)*

Other men live to eat, while I eat to live.
—*Socrates (469–399 B.C.)*

Tell me what you eat, and I will tell you what you are.
—*Anthelme Brillat-Savarin (1755–1826)*

Great eaters and great sleepers are incapable of anything else that is great.
—*Henri IV (1553–1610)*

Lunch kills half of Paris, supper the other half.
—*Charles de Secondat, Baron de Montesquieu (1689–1755)*

The Common Sense Manager

- realizes that carrying too many risk factors is as detrimental to his health as it is to his business

- exercises both body and soul

- sees both physical and mental fitness as *musts*

- regards physical exercise and reading as good long-term investments

- enjoys good food, but only in moderation

- does not need a power breakfast

- appreciates a tossed salad as the best power lunch available and never eats desserts

- is diet-conscious before he has to diet

CHARACTERISTIC 8

*"Having few but real friends"—Choosing friends
and foes carefully is always more difficult
than one might assume*

Building Friendships

Have no friends not equal to yourself.
— Confucius (c. 551–c. 479 B.C.)

Ignorance is always ready to admire itself; procure yourself
critical friends.
— Nicolas Boileau (1636–1711)

Between friends there is no need of justice.
— Aristotle (384-322 B.C.)

He that is neither one thing nor the other has no friends.
— Aesop (c. 550 B.C.)

Life becomes useless and insipid when we no longer have
either friends or enemies.
— Christina of Sweden (1626-1689)

Friends may come and go, but enemies accumulate.
— Thomas Jones (1916-1981)

Friendship is far more tragic than love. It lasts longer.
— Oscar Wilde (1854-1900)

The Common Sense Manager

- chooses his friends carefully

- knows that everybody's friend is nobody's friend

- values friendly advice, even if it is critical

- invests in friendship as he would in his business

- makes friends when he does not need them

- stresses *quid pro quo* in licensing, but not in personal
  relationships

CHARACTERISTIC 9

"Living now, not later"—Life is not a rehearsal

Enjoying Happiness

Most people work the greater part of their time for a mere living: and the little freedom which remains to them so troubles them that they use every means of getting rid of it.
—Johann Wolfgang von Goethe (1749–1832)

The shortness of life cannot dissuade us from its pleasures, nor console us for its pains.
—Luc de Clapiers, Marquis de Vauvenargues (1715–1747)

Happiness is an expression of the soul in considered actions.
—Aristotle (384–322 B.C.)

When we are unable to find tranquility within ourselves, it is useless to seek it elsewhere.
—François, Duc de La Rochefoucauld (1613–1680)

The Common Sense Manager:

- likes positive stress, reduces negative
- calls his wife, or significant other, from the office once in a while, even if there is no emergency
- takes his kids to the office from time to time
- tries to be himself rather than a role fulfiller
- knows that happiness depends on himself
- prefers his own way of life over Type A or Type B behavior

CHARACTERISTIC 10

"Relying on common sense"—Does not need a definition for common sense

Valuing Common Sense

More will be accomplished, and better, and with more ease, if every man does what he is best fitted to do, and nothing else.

— Plato (c. 428–348 B.C.)

There ain't nothin' as uncommon as common sense.

— Frank McKinney "Kin" Hubbard (1868–1950)

Common sense is the very antipode of science.

— Edward Bradford Titchener (1867–1927)

I can't read a book, but I can read de people.

— Sojourner Truth (c. 1797–1883)

Science is nothing but trained and organized common sense.

—Thomas Henry Huxley (1825–1895)

Do not be bullied out of your common sense by the specialist; two to one, he is a pedant.

— Oliver Wendell Holmes Jr. (1841–1935)

Sociology is the science with the greatest number of methods and the least results.

—Jules Henri Poincaré (1854–1912)

Taste is the common sense of genius.

François René, Vicomte de Chateaubriand (1768–1848)

The Common Sense Manager

- applies reason, judgment and common sense to his activities
- has an open heart and an open mind, and distrusts theoretical arguments
- relies on his experience and intuition as much as on computer printouts
- encourages and rewards personal initiative
- prefers common sense management to Theory X or Theory Y management
- values common sense even if it was "not invented here"

SUMMING UP

Common sense among men of fortune is rare.

—*Juvenal (fl. 1st to 2nd
century A.D.)*

Chapter 3

MANAGING WITH COMMON SENSE: THE MAIN TASKS

• • • • • • • • •

We have tried to identify the main ingredients of Common Sense Management: Holding to convictions, while tolerating ambiguity. Sustaining leadership and making decisions. Confronting risks and accepting criticism. Relishing change, while relying on experience. Accepting perceptions as reality and making effective use of one's own perceived personality. All these elements constitute important ingredients of Common Sense Management.

We then have looked at the *main characteristics* of a Common Sense Manager. He or she is a personality perfecter, accepts power as a responsibility, invests in people, relies on heart and head, respects both work and leisure, practices a healthy lifestyle, is in control of risk factors, builds lasting friendships, accepts happiness and values common sense as a guiding principle.

Common Sense Management by a Common Sense Manager requires the performance of a number of *tasks* which constitute the essentials of managing with common sense. Those tasks can be defined as follows:

- to envision the future *and* to set goals
- to decide on priorities *and* to evaluate progress
- to work sensibly *and* to manage time carefully
- to master communication *and* to explain explanations
- to understand theory *and* to remain practical

TASK 1

Know where you want to go. Otherwise it does not matter how well you proceed

Envisioning the Future

Never let the future disturb you. You will meet it, if you have to, with the same weapons of reason which today arm you against the present.
—Marcus Aurelius (121–180)

A mariner must have his eye upon rocks and sands, as well as upon the North Star.
—Thomas Fuller (1654–1734)

A man gazing at the stars is proverbially at the mercy of the puddles in the road.
—Alexander Smith (1830–1867)

Look up at the stars, but watch your steps in the dark alley.
— Friedrich Wilhelm Nietzsche (1844–1900)

Well it's a good thing to trust in Providence. But I believe the Almighty likes a little co-operation now and again.
— Frances Parkinson Keyes (1885–1970)

The Common Sense Manager

- does not act until he has a vision

- has a perspective which is "micro," but takes into account the overall "macro" situation

- knows that a global strategy may be chic, but that only effective local strategies can assure worldwide success

- makes strategic issue analysis the main part of any strategic planning exercise

- sees the acid test of strategic planning in the number of activities which will no longer be done in the future

- uses vision to build company culture

TASK 2

*Avoid a lack of goals. No goals
are worse than bad ones*

Setting Goals

Perfection of means and confusion of goals seems — in my opinion — to characterize our age. —*Albert Einstein (1879–1955)*

One never notices what has been done; one can only see what remains to be done. —*Marie Curie (1867–1937)*

The difficulty in life is the choice. —*George Moore (1852–1933)*

The secret of success is constancy in purpose.
—*Benjamin Disraeli, Earl of Beaconsfield (1804–1881)*

Practice yourself, for heaven's sake, in little things, and thence proceed to greater. —*Epictetus (c. 50–c. 138 A.D.)*

Delay is preferable to error. —*Thomas Jefferson (1743–1826)*

The Common Sense Manager

- knows that setting strategic goals is his major task
- has long-term decisions made by people who will still be present when their results mature
- focuses on the customer-competitor-technology triangle
- realizes that if he wants to be the best in too many areas, he is going to be average in all of them
- avoids going from analysis to paralysis
- may strive for increased market shares or increased profits, but never for both at the same time
- knows that getting quality work done in time, having a good working environment and enjoying job satisfaction in a participatory organization are more important goals for the individual than quantitative market shares, growth rates, structural percentages and ROI levels

TASK 3

*Set your priorities. Otherwise
somebody else will do it*

Deciding on Priorities

Never promise more than you can perform.
—Publilius Syrus (fl. 1st century B.C.)

To be a success in business, be daring, be first, be different.
—Henry Marchant (1741–1796)

I never lose an opportunity of urging a practical beginning, however small.
—Florence Nightingale (1820–1910)

The man of virtue makes the difficulty to be overcome his first business, and success only a subsequent consideration.
—Confucius (c. 551–c. 479 B.C.)

Take time to deliberate, but when the time for action has arrived, stop thinking and go in.
—Napoleon Bonaparte (1769–1821)

It is not only what we do, but also what we do not do, for which we are accountable.
—Molière (Jean Baptiste Poquelin) (1622–1673)

The Common Sense Manager

- does the important before the urgent

- knows what will have to be done next, before he decides on what needs to be done first

- believes in numerous second priorities and only in very few first priorities

- has a "to do" list of what not to do

- makes his priorities clearly known to other people

TASK 4

Measure progress to have it occur

Evaluating Progress

Progress needs the brakeman, but the brakeman should not spend all his time putting on the brakes.

— Elbert Hubbard (1856–1915)

Behold the turtle, he makes progress only when he sticks his neck out.

— James Bryant Conant (1893–1978)

Fanaticism is redoubling your effort when you have forgotten your aim.

— George Santayana (1863–1952)

It is through disobedience that progress has been made, through disobedience and rebellion.

— Oscar Wilde (1854–1900)

One must now apologize for any success in business as if it were a violation of the moral law, so that today it is worse to prosper than to be a criminal.

— Socrates (469–399 B.C.)

The Common Sense Manager

- never looks backwards into the future
- knows that progress tends to come in small steps rather than in big jumps
- measures progress as an output over time
- distinguishes progress from success
- sets progress-oriented reward systems
- concentrates on shaping company culture instead of analyzing stars, cash cows or dogs in his business portfolio

TASK 5

Work harder and smarter. But don't forget that there are other ways to enjoy life, too

Working Sensibly

Work and days were offered to us, and we chose work.
—Ralph Waldo Emerson (1803–1882)

A professional is one who does his best work when he feels
the least like working.
—Frank Lloyd Wright (1869–1959)

If all the year were playing holidays, to sport would be as
tedious as to work.
—William Shakespeare (1564–1616)

It is not hard work which is dreary; it is superficial work.
That is always boring in the long run.
—Edith Hamilton (1867–1963)

Work keeps us from three great evils, boredom, vice,
and need.
—Voltaire (François Marie Arouet) (1694–1778)

Nothing is to be had for nothing.
—Epictetus (c. 50–c. 138 A.D.)

If one works too much, one has no time to make money.
—Polish-Jewish proverb

The Common Sense Manager

- cherishes work, but is not a workaholic
- prefers good work to hard work
- sees working as a means, not as an end in itself
- is not afraid to profess a Puritan work ethic
- is not ashamed to enjoy well-deserved leisure, either
- works hard—and enjoys hard

TASK 6

Regard time as money. But be aware that only money
may be recovered if it is lost

Managing Time Carefully

Those who have most to do, and are willing to work, will find the most time.
— Samuel Smiles (1812–1904)

Remember that time is money.
— Benjamin Franklin (1706–1790)

I must govern the clock, not be governed by it.
— Golda Meir (1898–1978)

Those who work much do not work hard.
— Henry David Thoreau (1817–1862)

Those who make the worst use of their time are the first to complain of its brevity.
— Jean de La Bruyère (1645–1696)

Time flies, and what is past is done.
— Johann Wolfgang von Goethe (1749–1832)

Time is waste of money.
— Oscar Wilde (1854–1900)

The Common Sense Manager

- manages time like assets or people
- uses his time not as an expenditure, but as an investment
- sets starting and ending times for meetings, and sticks to both
- goes to see people rather than have them come to his office; they will be pleased, and he can leave at his discretion
- avoids saying "yes" under time pressure
- sets time aside to manage it

TASK 7

*Practice communication as a two-way exchange
that starts with listening*

Mastering Communication

Ideal conversation must be an exchange of thought and not an exhibition of wit or oratory.
— *Emily Post (1873–1960)*

In Paris they simply stared when I spoke to them in French. I never did succeed in making those idiots understand their own language.
— *Mark Twain (1835–1910)*

True eloquence consists in saying all that should be said, and that only.
— *François, Duc de La Rochefoucauld (1613–1680)*

The best orator is one who can make men see with their ears.
— *Arab proverb*

There are some who speak one moment before they think.
— *Jean de La Bruyère (1646–1696)*

Rhetoric is the art of ruling the minds of men.
Plato (c. 428–348 B.C.)

The Common Sense Manager

- speaks to the head, to the heart, to the guts
- reduces complexity to understandable images and meaningful examples
- knows that an adequate answer in time is much better than a perfect answer too late
- encourages people to say what they mean and to mean what they say
- realizes that if he tells the truth, he does not have to remember what he said
- communicates by listening
- points out that questions are never indiscreet, but answers might be
- recognizes that acknowledging, complimenting and thanking are powerful means of communicating

TASK 8

First, explain what you want to say. Then, say it.
After that, explain what you wanted to say

Explaining Explanations

I wish he would explain his explanation.
— *George Noel Gordon, Lord Byron (1788–1824)*

Understanding is the beginning of approving.
— *André Gide (1869–1951)*

One picture is worth more than a thousand words.
— *Chinese proverb*

Shallow understanding from people of goodwill is more frustrating than absolute understanding from people of ill-will.
— *Martin Luther King, Jr. (1929–1968)*

"Shut up," he explained.
— *Ring Lardner (1885–1933)*

The Common Sense Manager

- knows that little is self-explanatory
- manages attention rather than efforts by explanation
- understands jargon, but does not use it
- sees explanation as problem-solving information
- recognizes the need to explain core values and principles, if he or she wants to push decision-making and authority effectively down the line
- explains, explains, explains

TASK 9

Never forget that scientists do scientific work not just for the common good, but also because they like it

Plain Dealing with Theory and Science

The whole of science is nothing more than a refinement of everyday thinking.
—Albert Einstein (1879–1955)

There are in fact two things, science and opinion; the former begets knowledge, the latter ignorance.
—Hippocrates (c. 460–c. 370 B.C.)

What is false in the science of facts may be true in the science of values.
—George Santayana (1863–1952)

Science is built of facts the way a house is built of bricks; but an accumulation of facts is no more science than a pile of bricks is a house.
—Jules Henri Poincaré (1854–1912)

Evidence drawn empirically from facts, though it may justify the action of the practical man, is not scientifically conclusive.
—Beatrice Potter Webb (1858–1943)

The outcome of any serious research can only be to make two questions grow where only one grew before.
—Thorstein Veblen (1857–1929)

It is a very sad thing that nowadays there is so little useless information.
—Oscar Wilde (1854–1900)

The Common Sense Manager

- sees an important goal of science as generating new knowledge which will satisfy needs in the marketplace
- deals with science in the context of ethics and values
- makes researchers meet real customers from time to time
- gives scientists a bit less freedom than they request, but as much as they deserve
- handles research budgets with the same care and attention as marketing expenditures

TASK 10

If you are still confused, but on a higher level,
step down and admit it

Remaining Practical

Learn, compare, collect the facts.
> — *Ivan Petrovich Pavlov (1849–1936)*

Saddle your dreams afore you ride 'em.
> — *Mary Webb (1881–1927)*

There are people who are socialists and rebels today and company directors tomorrow.
> — *Friedrich Hebbel (1813–1863)*

One of the things being in politics has taught me is that men are not a reasoned or reasonable sex.
> — *Margaret Thatcher (1925–)*

Good women always think it is their fault when someone else is being offensive. Bad women never take the blame for anything.
> — *Anita Brookner (1938–)*

Never practice what you preach. If you are going to practice it, why preach it?
> — *Lincoln Steffens (1866–1936)*

Practice yourself, for heaven's sake, in little things; and thence proceed to greater.
> — *Epictetus (c. 50–c. 138 A.D.)*

Think globally, act locally.
> — *René Dubos (1901–1982)*

The Common Sense Manager

- does not get confused by theoretical arguments
- seeks simplicity, but distrusts it
- prefers two-page memos to dissertations
- is more impressed by sound logic than by the length of publication lists
- seldom has time for footnotes
- is not afraid to ask practical questions

SUMMING UP

Nothing astonishes men so much as
common sense and plain dealing.

— *Ralph Waldo Emerson (1803–1882)*

Chapter 4

COMMON SENSE INSIDE THE ORGANIZATON: THE MAIN INSIGHTS

• • • • • • • • • •

Common Sense Management relies on a set of fundamental principles. The Common Sense Manager is a person with a number of particular characteristics. Managing with Common Sense describes the performance of a set of basic tasks. This triangle has to interact both with the inside of an organization and with its external environment.

Modern management wisdom tends to imply that primary attention has to be given to what lies outside the organization. It is true, environment, markets and customers are important. No organization will eventually flourish, or even survive, if it does not find its justification in the outside world by offering products or services for which there are markets and needs.

Giving prime emphasis to the outside world, however, may lead to an under-estimation of the "tender loving care" which the organization itself requires so as best to perform its desired functions.

A commonsensical approach suggests that *fifty percent attention be given to the inside of the organization,* fifty percent to its outside. When this is done, a number of "insights" and "outsights" become apparent.

The "insights" are that it makes common sense:

- to deal with people
- to refine interpersonal skills
- to be interested in innovation
- to use experts carefully
- to be smart with lawyers
- to plan and budget with a purpose
- to second-guess number-crunchers
- to understand bureaucracy
- to keep a lean organization
- to combine quality with productivity

INSIGHT 1

*Spending an inordinate amount of time on recruiting is
a very good way of getting, if not the best, at least
the most appropriate people*

Emphasizing People Management

The most valuable executive is one who is training
somebody to be a better man than he is.
—Robert G. Ingersoll (1833–1899)

You can accomplish by kindness what you cannot do by force.
—Publilius Syrus (fl. 1st century B.C.)

We ought not to treat living creatures like shoes or household
belongings, which when worn with use we throw away.
—Plutarch (c. 46–c. 120 A.D.)

As a general rule, remuneration by fixed salaries does not in
any class of functionaries produce the maximum of zeal.
—John Stuart Mill (1806–1873)

Abused soil brings forth stunted growths.
—Margaret Sanger (1883–1966)

People who make no noise are dangerous.
—Jean de La Fontaine (1621–1695)

The Common Sense Manager

- knows that personal selection is decisive, since people
  count more than anything else in business
- deals not only with explicit day-to-day decisions, but also with
  the emotional needs, hopes and ideas of his subordinates
- uses reward/punishment systems which are clear to
  everybody
- rewards intra-organizational maneuvering less than
  sensible risk-taking in the marketplace
- tries constantly to strengthen his subordinates by providing
  meaningful work, challenging career opportunities and a
  rewarding work environment
- encourages outspokenness
- relies on trust rather than on control
- is willing to fire or downgrade people when they are not
  doing their job

INSIGHT 2

*If you take people the way they are, you are not
likely to get better ones*

Refining Interpersonal Skills

The best executive is the one who has sense enough to pick good men to do what he wants done, and self-restraint enough to keep from meddling with them while they do it.

—Theodore Roosevelt (1858–1919)

I sit here all day trying to persuade people to do the things they ought to have sense enough to do without my persuading them.

—Harry S. Truman (1884–1972)

The ability to deal with people is as purchasable a commodity as sugar or coffee, and I pay more for that ability than for any other under the sun. *—John Davison Rockefeller (1839–1937)*

What a man dislikes in his superiors, let him not display in the treatment of his inferiors. *—Tseng-tzu (fl. 5th century B.C.)*

It is frequently a misfortune to have very brilliant men in charge of affairs; they expect too much of ordinary men.

—Thucydides (c. 460–c. 400 B.C.)

The Common Sense Manager

- enjoys dealing with people
- treats first-class people first class, whether they are customers, colleagues or subordinates
- does not distinguish between male and female managers, but between professionals and non-professionals
- induces in his people a sense of belonging and pride in being a member of the team
- knows that he cannot expect loyalty from below if he doesn't first provide loyalty from above
- must be willing to punish incompetence or disloyalty as well as reward creativity and steadfastness

INSIGHT 3

*No industry is so mature that it no longer
needs to innovate*

Being Interested in Innovation

Inventors and men of genius have almost always been regarded as fools at the beginning (and very often at the end) of their careers.

— Feodor Mikhailovich Dostoevsky (1821–1881)

No man was ever great by imitation.

— Samuel Johnson (1709–1784)

What appears on the surface, is almost never the truth.

— Marie Madeleine de La Fayette (1634–1693)

To do just the opposite is also a form of imitation.

— Georg Christoph Lichtenberg (1742–1799)

Imitation is the sincerest form of flattery.

— Charles Caleb Colton (1780–1832)

The Common Sense Manager

- fosters innovation as a form of survival

- welcomes imitation, because it forces him to innovate

- wants innovation not just from the R&D people

- knows that innovation comes from dealing with the customer, and therefore cannot be delegated upwards

- helps innovative problem-solving by issue definition, coalition building and resource mobilization

INSIGHT 4

Choose good experts, not friendly ones

Using Experts Carefully

How quick come the reasons for approving what we like!
—Jane Austen (1775–1817)

No man can be a pure specialist without being, in a strict sense, an idiot.
— George Bernard Shaw (1856–1950)

Science is a first-rate piece of furniture for a man's upper-chamber, if he has common-sense on the ground floor.
— Oliver Wendell Holmes, Sr. (1809–1894)

It is better, of course, to know useless things than to know nothing.
— Lucius Annaeus Seneca (c. 4 B.C.–65 A.D.)

If we value the pursuit of knowledge we must be free to follow wherever that search may lead us.
—Adlai Ewing Stevenson (1900–1965)

We search for truth and only find uncertainty within ourselves.
— Blaise Pascal (1623–1662)

The Common Sense Manager

- treats an expert as a man who has made all the mistakes which are possible in his field of knowledge

- prefers experience to expertise

- distinguishes facts from opinions

- chooses experts for independent advice rather than to reinforce personal prejudices

- does not accept an expert who will not admit his own fallibility

INSIGHT 5

*Lawyers are meant to help you run the business,
not to run the business*

Being Smart with Lawyers

The first thing we do, let's kill all the lawyers.
—William Shakespeare (1564–1616)

Of the professions, it may be said that soldiers are becoming too popular, parsons too lazy, physicians too mercenary, and lawyers too powerful. *— Charles Caleb Colton (1780–1832)*

If there were no bad people there would be no good lawyers.
—Charles Dickens (1812–1870)

A lean compromise is better than a fat lawsuit.
—George Herbert (1593–1633)

The law, it is an ass. *—Charles Dickens (1812–1870)*

The man who sees both sides of a question is a man who sees absolutely nothing at all. *—Oscar Wilde (1854–1900)*

What is the answer?. . . In that case, what is the question?
Gertrude Stein (1874–1946)

The Common Sense Manager

- listens to legal arguments, but uses his own judgment to run the business
- when seeking outside advice, uses lawyers who are not yet partners in their law firm
- does not always fall for the liability scare
- knows that the anti-trust argument may be just another excuse for not doing an in-depth analysis
- refuses to accept "on the one hand, on the other hand" advice
- asks for percentages of win/lose probabilities, instead of lengthy opinions

INSIGHT 6

Control the planners. Otherwise they
will control you

Purposeful Planning and Budgeting

A bad plan it is that admits of no modification.
— Publilius Syrus (fl. 1st century B.C.)

The more human beings proceed by plan the more
effectively they may be hit by accident.
— Friedrich Dürrenmatt (1921–)

Take time to deliberate, but when the time for action has
arrived, stop thinking and go in.
— Napoleon Bonaparte (1769–1821)

Perfection of planning is a symptom of decay. During a
period of exciting discovery or progress, there is no time to
plan the perfect headquarters. The time for that comes later,
when all the important work has been done.
— Cyril Northcote Parkinson (1909–)

What people say you cannot do, you try and find that
you can.
— Henry David Thoreau (1817–1862)

The Common Sense Manager

- understands planning as an education process rather than
  as a numbers game
- forces planners to meet real customers again and again
- sees the first task of planning as disaggregating complexity
- is ratio-conscious, but total-contribution-driven
- knows that profits are earned in currencies, not in percentages
- is aware that too much MIS management can become
  mismanagement
- uses zero-base budgeting to abolish all services which
  profit only the people who render them
- uses historical accounting data in the same way he uses his
  rear mirror when driving the car—only on straight roads,
  or when backing up

INSIGHT 7

*The invention of Lotus 1-2-3 should not
substitute sensitivity analysis for
sound reasoning and judgment*

Second-Guessing Number Crunchers

It doesn't help to remember the price of yesterday's roast beef.
— Ben Jonson (1572–1637)

The success of any great moral enterprise does not depend upon numbers.
—William Lloyd Garrison (1805–1879)

Nothing that costs only a dollar is worth having.
— Elizabeth Arden (1878–1966)

What we obtain too cheaply, we esteem too lightly; it is dearness only which gives everything its value.
—Thomas Paine (1737–1809)

What is a cynic? A man who knows the price of everything and the value of nothing.
— Oscar Wilde (1854–1900)

The theory of probabilities is at bottom nothing but common sense reduced to calculus.
— Pierre Simon de Laplace (1749–1827)

If a man has money, it is usually a sign that he knows how to take care of it.
— Edgar Watson Howe (1853–1937)

The Common Sense Manager

- looks behind the numbers
- knows the difference between bookkeepers and management accountants
- never asks more than three "what if" questions
- prefers accuracy to precision, despite the invention of spreadsheets
- searches for plausibility and fair balance
- leverages his knowledge base as much as he does his company
- makes sure that the costs of control do not exceed the value of the attainable benefits

INSIGHT 8

*Bureaucracy is the only real threat to both glasnost
and entrepreneurship*

Understanding Bureaucracy

The length of a meeting rises with the square of the number of people present.

—Eileen Shanahan (1924–)

The more laws, the more offenders.

—Thomas Fuller (1654–1734)

Forms are for mediocrity, and it is fortunate that mediocrity can act only according to routine. Ability takes its flight unhindered.

—Napoleon Bonaparte (1769–1821)

The organization of any bureaucracy is very much like a septic tank. The really big chunks always rise to the top.

—John Imhoff (1923–)

The Common Sense Manager

- knows that bureaucracies deal in power, companies in markets; therefore, he manages bureaucracy from the top down, markets from the bottom up

- provides the bureaucrat with the answer to the question which will be asked by his superior; gives to the market the answer which will solve the need of the customer

- uses committees for information-sharing and culture-building, but never for decision-making

- makes sure that people want to be coordinated, before he establishes a coordination committee

- fights bureaucracy by rewarding risk takers

- never puts entrepreneurs and bureaucrats into the same organization

- recalls that a common epitaph of bureaucrats is, "He failed to consult"

INSIGHT 9

The dinosaurs may have died out because they grew too heavy to search for food. Fat organizations risk the same fate

Keeping a Lean Organization

We tend to meet any new situation by reorganizing. It can be a wonderful method for creating the illusion of progress while producing inefficiency and demoralization.
—Petronius (died c. 66 A.D.)

Unhappy the general who comes on the field of battle with a system.
—Napoleon Bonaparte (1769–1821)

Distrust all systematizers, and avoid them. The will to a system shows a lack of honesty.
—Friedrich Wilhelm Nietzsche (1844–1900)

I have found that the brown bears are under the jurisdiction of the Secretary of Agriculture, the grizzly bears under the care of the Secretary of Interior, and the polar bears under my protection as Secretary of Commerce.
—Herbert Clark Hoover (1874–1964)

The Common Sense Manager

- knows committees are groups which keep minutes and lose hours

- puts the emphasis in a working party on working rather than on party

- balances economies of scale with the diseconomies of coordination

- avoids the danger of substituting process for substance

- finds the right balance between conformity and disobedience, between order and chaos

- drops an existing task before adding on a new one in an organization

INSIGHT 10

*Quality, like productivity, can be improved only
by people. Provide them with the right incentives
and they will achieve it*

Combining Quality with Productivity

Give them quality. That is the best kind of advertising.
—Milton S. Hershey (1857–1945)

The surest foundation of a manufacturing concern is quality. After that, and a long way after, comes cost.
—Andrew Carnegie (1835–1919)

It is quality rather than quantity that matters.
—Lucius Annaeus Seneca (c. 4 B.C.–65 A.D.)

A company cannot increase its productivity. People can.
—Robert Half (1918–)

The Common Sense Manager

- knows that quality is hard to maintain, easy to destroy
- views quality as meeting customer needs and expectations
- is convinced that quality pays, but is aware that too much quality costs
- combines quality with productivity
- prefers quality circles to cost-cutting committees
- measures productivity improvements to make them happen

SUMMING UP

Common sense suits itself to the ways of
the world. Wisdom tries to conform to
the ways of heaven.

—Joseph Joubert (1754–1824)

Chapter 5

COMMON SENSE IN MANAGING THE OUTSIDE WORLD: THE MAIN OUTSIGHTS

•   •   •   •   •   •   •   •   •   •

Investing time in people, giving them personal attention, fostering innovation, dealing efficiently with experts, lawyers, planners, accountants and other number crunchers, mastering bureaucracy by keeping a lean organization and combining quality with productivity are, as has been pointed out, essential components of applying common sense *inside* an organization.

An equal amount of energy, time and common sense is, however, also necessary for successfully dealing with what lies *outside* the organization—its environment, both natural and competitive. The outside forces which an organization is confronted with, the competitive pressures it has to face, and the market and customer needs which it has to understand successfully demand the application of common sense as well. The formula should be: *half of the efforts to the inside, the other half to the outside.*

Some important "outsights" for common sense in managing the outside world would appear to be:

- to inquire into markets and customers
- to engage in competition
- to take account of public opinion
- to play politics
- to work with the media
- to appreciate exposure
- to respect the law
- to be guided by one's own conscience
- to practice ethics

91

OUTSIGHT 1

*An organization performs best if it satisfies the
needs of markets and customers.
Clarify those needs*

Inquiring into Markets and Customers

The customer is always right.
— H. Gordon Selfridge (1864–1947)

The business world worships mediocrity. Officially we revere free enterprise, initiative and individuality. Unofficially we fear it.
— George Lois (1931–)

It is not the going out of port, but the coming in, that determines the success of a voyage.
— Henry Ward Beecher (1813–1887)

The very first step towards success in any occupation is to become interested in it.
—William Osler (1849–1919)

If we value the pursuit of knowledge, we must be free to follow wherever that search may lead us.
—Adlai Ewing Stevenson (1900–1965)

The Common Sense Manager

- distinguishes know-how from know-why
- reads about megatrends, but is concerned about the relevant microtrends impacting on his business
- tries first to understand the problem before offering a solution
- restricts quantitative market research in favor of qualitative customer surveys
- distrusts high market share numbers, since they usually reflect too narrow a definition of the relevant market
- prefers marketing people in the research department to research people in the marketing department
- listens to the echo behind the door

OUTSIGHT 2

*Competition works, either for you
or against you*

Engaging in Competition

Do as adversaries do in law. Strive mightily, but eat and drink as friends.
—William Shakespeare (1564–1616)

I feel sorry for men—they have more problems than women. In the first place they have to compete with women.
—Françoise Sagan (1935–)

Once a woman is made man's equal, she becomes his superior.
—Margaret Thatcher (1925–)

If you pay peanuts, you get monkeys.
—James Goldsmith (1933–)

It is relatively easy to fix prices that are already fixed.
—John Kenneth Galbraith (1908–)

You must lose a fly to catch a trout.
—George Herbert (1593–1633)

Thou shalt not covet, but tradition approves all forms of competition.
—Arthur Hugh Clough (1819–1861)

The Common Sense Manager

- believes in competition, even when it hurts
- welcomes competition as a way of keeping an organization on its toes
- knows that one can compete in quality and service, not just in price
- looks at what the competition is doing and then does it differently
- realizes that friendly competitors are either not friendly or no competitors
- emphasizes that quality and service are important elements of competition, and that they can be assured only by people

OUTSIGHT 3

*Public opinion is an important element of success
or failure in business*

Taking Account of Public Opinion

Public opinion only exists where there are no ideas.
— *Oscar Wilde (1854–1900)*

Every man speaks of public opinion, and means by public opinion, public opinion minus his opinion.
— *Gilbert Keith Chesterton (1874–1936)*

Public opinion is no more than this: what people think that other people think.
— *Alfred Austin (1835–1913)*

That mysterious independent variable of political calculation, public opinion.
— *Thomas Henry Huxley (1825–1895)*

In America, public opinion is the leader.
— *Frances Perkins (1882–1965)*

There are times when the belief of the people, though it may be without ground, is as significant as the truth.
— *Friedrich von Schiller (1759–1805)*

Public opinion is the thermometer a monarch should constantly consult.
— *Napoleon Bonaparte (1769–1821)*

We are ruled by public opinion, not by statute-law.
— *Elbert Hubbard (1856–1915)*

The Common Sense Manager

- always takes account of public opinion
- monitors changes in public opinion
- sees public opinion as an important source of power
- knows that public opinion is determined more by feelings than by intellect
- tries to change, but not fight, public opinion
- uses polls, not newspapers, to detect important trends in public opinion
- knows that public opinion is fickle and can change instantly

OUTSIGHT 4

Industry is part of society. Society is part of politics. Therefore, politics always sets the context for any business

Playing Politics with a Purpose

Politics is not an exact science.
> — *Otto von Bismarck (1815–1898)*

Man is by nature a political animal.
> —*Aristotle (384–322 B.C.)*

Practical politics consists in ignoring facts.
> — *Henry Adams (1838–1918)*

The justification of majority rule in politics is not to be found in its ethical superiority.
> —*Walter Lippmann (1889–1974)*

In our age there is no such thing as "keeping out of politics." All issues are political issues.
> — *George Orwell (1903–1950)*

These are my politics: to change what we can; to better what we can; but still to bear in mind that man is but a devil weakly fettered by some generous beliefs and impositions.
> — *Robert Louis Stevenson (1850–1894)*

The Common Sense Manager

- is politically active and visible
- establishes good personal relationships with political opinion leaders
- invests as much in ruling parties as he does in the opposition
- understands political processes inside and outside the company
- realizes that the political environment outside the company will always impact on his business

OUTSIGHT 5

*As long as people read newspapers and watch
television, the media will play a decisive
role in every facet of business*

Working with the Media

Bad news travels fast and far.
— *Plutarch (c. 46–c. 120 A.D.)*

When a dog bites a man that is not news, but when a man bites a dog, that is news.
— *John B. Bogart (1845–1921)*

Four hostile newspapers are more to be feared than a thousand bayonets.
— *Napoleon Bonaparte (1769–1821)*

Our words have wings, but fly not where we would.
— *George Eliot (1819–1880)*

News is the first rough draft in history.
— *Benjamin Crowninshield Bradlee (1921–)*

Never lose your temper with the press or the public, is a major rule of political life.
— *Christabel Pankhurst (1880–1958)*

The Common Sense Manager

- realizes that there is no good news or bad news, only interesting or dull news
- knows that the press has a bottom line, which is called circulation
- gets to know good journalists at a time when he does not need them
- tries to influence journalists only by providing them with a better story
- finds out what makes a story interesting before he is part of it
- distinguishes favorable/unfavorable stories from accurate/inaccurate reports
- calls the reporter, not the editor, if he is not pleased with a press story
- calls the editor if the reporter has done a superior job
- thinks carefully before issuing rebuttals, since they bring him into the limelight twice

OUTSIGHT 6

*Moving means progressing. Nobody achieves
anything by standing still. He who
moves gets exposed*

Appreciating Exposure

We live under a government of men and morning newspapers.
—Wendell Phillips (1811–1884)

The medium is the message.
—Marshall Herbert McLuhan (1911–1980)

The circulation of ideas is, of all kinds of commerce, the one whose benefits are most certain.
—Germaine de Staël (1766–1817)

It is a rough road that leads to the heights of greatness.
—Lucius Annaeus Seneca (c. 4 B.C.–65 A.D.)

The man who occupies the first place seldom plays the principal part.
—Johann Wolfgang von Goethe (1749–1832)

Publicity, publicity, publicity, is the greatest moral factor and force in our public life.
—Joseph Pulitzer (1847–1911)

The Common Sense Manager

- knows that visibility counts in business
- enjoys substituting his face for the company logo
- has read and understood both Marx and Machiavelli
- prefers live interviews to taped statements
- knows that the media instinctively smells fear and dishonesty
- aspires not to be loved, but respected for his exposure

OUTSIGHT 7

*Respect the law, but don't always follow
the advice of lawyers*

Respecting the Law

Nobody has a more sacred obligation to obey the law than those who make the law.
— Sophocles (494–406 B.C.)

Laws too gentle are seldom obeyed; too severe, seldom executed.
— Benjamin Franklin (1706–1790)

The science of legislation is like that of medicine in one respect: that it is far more easy to point out what will do harm than what will do good.
— Charles Caleb Colton (1780–1832)

The more laws and order are made prominent, the more thieves and robbers there will be.
— Lao-tzu (c. 604–c. 531 B.C.)

The life of the law has not been logic: it has been experience.
— Oliver Wendell Holmes, Jr. (1841–1935)

A kingdom founded on injustice never lasts.
— Lucius Annaeus Seneca (c. 4 B.C.–65 A.D.)

The highest virtue is always against the law.
— Ralph Waldo Emerson (1803–1882)

The Common Sense Manager

- knows and respects the law
- has no fear of interpreting the law in his favor
- has his own set of rules which are complementary to the law
- is legal-minded, but not legalistic
- distinguishes between legally admissible and ethically justifiable practices

OUTSIGHT 8

A good conscience is the best memory

Acting in Conscience

The measure of any man's virtue is what he would do, if he had neither the laws nor public opinion, nor even his own prejudices, to control him.
—*William Hazlitt (1778–1830)*

Nowadays truth is the greatest news.
—*Thomas Fuller (1608–1661)*

Even when there is no law, there is conscience.
—*Publilius Syrus (fl. 1st century B.C.)*

The truth is rarely pure and never simple.
—*Oscar Wilde (1854–1900)*

Art, like morality, consists in drawing the line somewhere.
—*Gilbert Keith Chesterton (1874–1936)*

A man may not transgress the bounds of major morals, but may make errors in minor morals.
—*Confucius (c. 551–c. 479 B.C.)*

A leader who doesn't hesitate before he sends his nation into battle is not fit to be a leader.
—*Golda Meir (1898–1978)*

The moral sense teaches us what is right, and how to avoid it—when unpopular.
—*Mark Twain (1835–1910)*

The Common Sense Manager

- asks his conscience for guidance
- avoids activities of which his family would not approve
- realizes that he should always be able to stand public scrutiny
- knows that hiding something is more cumbersome than not doing it
- accepts that he will be judged by today's standards for what he did years ago, and knows that what he does today will be judged by standards not yet clearly articulated

OUTSIGHT 9

*The acid test of ethical standards is
their implementation*

Practicing Ethics

True wisdom consists in not departing from nature and in molding our conduct according to her laws and model.
— *Lucius Annaeus Seneca (c. 4 B.C.–65 A.D.)*

Do not seek dishonest gains: dishonest gains are losses.
— *Hesiod (fl. 8th century B.C.)*

God does not pay at the end of every week, but he pays.
— *Anne of Austria (1601–1666)*

Hold faithfulness and sincerity as first principles.
— *Confucius (c. 551–c. 479 B.C.)*

Never esteem anything as of advantage to you that will make you break your word or lose your self-respect.
— *Marcus Aurelius (121–180 A.D.)*

A successful man loses no reputation.
— *Thomas Fuller (1608–1661)*

Ethics is in origin that art of recommending to others the sacrifices required for co-operation with oneself.
— *Bertrand Russell (1872–1970)*

The Common Sense Manager

- knows that ethical behavior has its costs, but is convinced that they are eventually outweighed by its benefits
- is more concerned about long-term success and survival than about quarterly earnings
- has more important aims in business life than saving taxes
- sees good profits as good social responsibility, and *vice versa*
- does not use the argument of local customs or competitive standards to justify ethically questionable business practices
- emphasizes ethics in action more than ethics in textbooks
- knows that not everything legal is also legitimate
- realizes that present legal standards usually represent ethical expectations of five years ago

SUMMING UP

Honesty is largely a matter of information, of knowing that dishonesty is a mistake.

—*Edgar Watson Howe (1853–1937)*

THE COMMON SENSE
MANAGER'S CREDO

Cogito ergo sum.

— *René Descartes (1596–1650)*

•   •   •   •   •   •   •   •   •

SOME AFTERTHOUGHTS

The same common sense which makes an author write good things, makes him dread they are not good enough to deserve reading.

— *Jean de La Bruyère (1645–1696)*

I hate quotations. Tell me what you know.

— *Ralph Waldo Emerson (1803–1882)*

AN INDEX OF AUTHORS
With Some of Their Major Works

Acton, John Emerich Edward, Lord (1834–1902). English historian, moralist and philosopher.

Adams, Henry (1838–1918). American historian and man of letters. Author of *Mont-Saint-Michel and Chartres* (1904) and *The Education of Henry Adams* (1906).

Aesop (c. 550 B.C.). Greek fabulist.

Ali, Muhammed (1942–). American boxer.

Anne of Austria (1601–1666). Queen and regent of France.

Arden, Elizabeth (1878–1966). American cosmetics magnate.

Arendt, Hannah (1906–1975). German-American philosopher and historian.

Aristotle (384–322 B.C.). Greek philosopher, logician and scientist. Author of *Nicomachean Ethics* and *Politics*.

Austen, Jane (1775–1817). English novelist. Author of *Pride and Prejudice* (1813).

Austin, Alfred (1835–1913). English poet laureate. Author of *A Garden That I Love* (1894, 1907).

Beecher, Henry Ward (1813–1887). American liberal Congregational minister. Author of *Proverbs from Plymouth Pulpit* (1887).

Billings, Josh (1818–1885). American humorist. Author of *Farmer's Allminax* (1869–80).

Birkett, William Norman, Lord (1883–1962). English barrister and judge.

Bismarck, Otto von (1815–1898). German statesman; founder and first Chancellor of the German Empire.

Bogart, John B. (1845–1921). City Editor of the *New York Sun* (1873–90).

Boileau, Nicolas (1636–1711). French poet and literary critic. Author of *Against Women* (1694).

Bonaparte, Napoleon (1769–1821). French general and emperor.

Boren, James H. (1925–). American politician and writer.

Bradlee, Benjamin Crowningshield (1921–). American journalist. Author of *Conversations with Kennedy* (1975).

Brillat-Savarin, Anthelme (1755–1826). French lawyer, economist and gastronomist. Author of *The Physiology of Taste* (1825).

Brookner, Anita (1938–). British novelist.

Butler, Samuel (1835–1902). English novelist, essayist, translator and critic. Author of *The Way of All Flesh* (1903).

Byron, George Noel Gordon, Lord (1788–1824). English poet and satirist. Author of *The Corsair* (1814), *Childe Harold* (1816) and *Don Juan* (1819–24).

Carlyle, Thomas (1795–1881). Scottish essayist and historian. Author of *The French Revolution* (1837) and *Past and Present* (1843).

Carnegie, Andrew (1835–1919). American industrialist and philanthropist. Author of "The Gospel of Wealth" (1889).

Chanel, Coco (1883–1971). French couturier.

Chateaubriand, François René, Vicomte de (1768–1848). French diplomat and Romantic writer. Author of *The Genius of Christianity* (1802).

Chesterfield, Philip D.S., Earl of (1694–1773). English statesman and diplomat. Author of *Letters to His Illegitimate Son* (pub. 1774) and *Letters to His Godson* (pub. 1890).

Chesterton, Gilbert Keith (1874–1936). English poet, essayist, novelist and short story writer. Author of *All Things Considered* (1908), *The Man Who Was Thursday* (1908), *Orthodoxy* (1908) and the Father Brown mystery stories (1911–35).

Christie, Agatha (1891–1976). English mystery novelist.

Christina of Sweden (1626–1689). Queen of Sweden.

Churchill, Winston L.S. (1874–1965). Prime Minister of Great Britain (1940–45); statesman, orator and writer. Author of *The Second World War* (1948–53).

Cicero, Marcus Tullius (106–43 B.C.). Roman statesman, orator and Stoic philosopher. Author of *De Republica*.

Clough, Arthur Hugh (1819–1861). English poet.

Colton, Charles Caleb (1780–1832). English writer and clergyman.

Conant, James Bryant (1893–1978). American educator, president of Harvard University, scientist and diplomat. Author of *Modern Science and Modern Man* (1952) and *My Several Lives* (1970).

Confucius (c. 551–c. 479 B.C.). Chinese philosopher. Author of *Analects*.

Curie, Marie (1867–1934). French chemist, physicist and Nobel Prize winner (1903).

Descartes, René (1596–1650). French mathematician and philosopher. Author of *Discourse on Method* (1637), *Meditations on First Philosophy* (1641) and *The Principles of Philosophy* (1644).

Dewey, John (1859–1952). American philosopher, psychologist and educator. Author of *The School and Society* (1899), *Experience and Nature* (1925) and *Freedom and Culture* (1930).

Dickens, Charles John Huffman (1812–1870). English novelist. Author of *The Pickwick Papers* (1837), *Oliver Twist* (1837–39), *A Christmas Carol* (1843), *David Copperfield* (1835) and *Great Expectations* (1861).

Dietrich, Marlene (1901–). German-American actress.

Disraeli, Benjamin, Earl of Beaconsfield (1804–1881). English statesman and novelist; twice Prime Minister of Great Britian. Author of *Vivian Grey* (1826) and *Coningsby* (1844).

Dostoevsky, Feodor Mikhailovich (1821–1881). Russian novelist. Author of *Poor Folk* (1846), *Crime and Punishment* (1866), *The Idiot* (1868-69) and *The Brothers Karamazov* (1880).

Douglas, William O. (1898–1980). American jurist and Supreme Court Justice. Author of *An Almanac of Liberty* (1954) and *A Living Bill of Rights* (1961).

Drabble, Margaret (1939–). English novelist and critic. Author of *The Needle's Eye* (1972); editor of *The Oxford Companion to English Literature* (1985).

Dubos, René (1901–1982). French-American microbiologist. Author of *So Human an Animal* (1968).

Dürrenmatt, Friedrich (1921–). Swiss playwright. Author of *The Visit* (1958).

Einstein, Albert (1879–1955). German-American physicist and Nobel Prize winner (1921). Author of *Relativity: The Special and General Theory* (1918) and *The World as I See It* (1934).

Eliot, Charles W. (1834–1926). American chemist, educator and president of Harvard University.

Eliot, George (1819–1880). English novelist. Author of *Silas Marner* (1861) and *Middlemarch* (1872).

Elizabeth I (1533–1603). Queen of England.

Ellis, Havelock (1859–1939). English psychologist. Author of *Studies in the Psychology of Sex* (1897–1928).

Emerson, Ralph Waldo (1803–1882). American essayist, poet and lecturer. Author of *Essays* (1841; 1844) and *Representative Men* (1850).

Epictetus (c. 50–c. 138 A.D.). Phrygian Stoic philosopher. Author of the *Discourses*.

Euripides (c. 480–c. 405 B.C.). Greek tragic poet. Author of *Medea* (431), *Electra* (413) and *The Bacchae* (405).

Fields, W.C. (1880–1946). American comedian and actor.

Fitzgerald, F. Scott (1896–1940). American novelist and short story writer. Author of *The Great Gatsby* (1925).

Franklin, Benjamin (1706–1790). American statesman, writer, inventor, printer and scientist. Helped draft the Declaration of Independence. Author of *Poor Richard's Almanac* (1732–57).

Fuller, Thomas (1608–1661). English clergyman. Author of *History of the Worthies of England* (1662).

Fuller, Thomas, M.D. (1654–1734). English physician, writer and compiler. Author of *Gnomologia* (1732).

Gabor, Zsa Zsa (1919–). American actress.

Galbraith, John Kenneth (1908–). American economist. Author of *American Capitalism: The Concept of Countervailing Power* (1952) and *The Affluent Society* (1958).

Gandhi, Indira (1917–1987). Prime Minister of India.

Garrison, William Lloyd (1805–1879). American journalist and abolitionist. Publisher of the newspaper *Liberator* (1831-65).

Gide, André (1869-1951). French writer and Nobel Prize winner (1947). Author of *The Immoralist* (1902) and *The Counterfeiters* (1926).

Goethe, Johann Wolfgang von (1749–1832). German poet, playwright, novelist and scientist. Author of *The Sorrows of Young Werther* (1774) and *Faust* (Part I, 1808; Part II, 1832).

Goldsmith, James, Sir (1933–). English industrialist, active in international mergers and acquisitions.

Goldwyn, Samuel (1882–1974). American movie producer and founder of Metro-Goldwyn-Mayer.

Gracián, Baltasar (1601–1658). Spanish philosopher, scholar, satirist, novelist and epigrammatist. Author of *The Hero* (1637) and *El Criticón* (1651–57).

Half, Robert (1918–). American personnel recruiter, executive and franchiser. Author of *Robert Half on Hiring* (1985).

Hamilton, Edith (1867–1963). American writer and educator. Author of *The Greek Way* (1930).

Hazlitt, William (1778–1830). English essayist. Author of *Table Talk* (1821–22) and *Spirit of the Age* (1825).

Hebbel, Friedrich (1813–1863). German playwright. Author of *Judith* (1840) and *The Nibelung Trilogy* (1862).

Henry IV of France (1553–1610). First Bourbon King of France.

Heraclitus (c. 535–c. 475 B.C.). Greek philosopher. Author of *Cosmic Fragments*.

Herbert, George (1593–1633). English Metaphysical poet. Author of *The Temple* (1633).

Herodotus (c. 485–425 B.C.). Greek historian. Author of *The Histories*.

Hershey, Milton S. (1857–1945). American manufacturer and philanthropist; founder of the Hershey Chocolate Corporation.

Hesiod (fl. eighth century B.C.). Greek poet. Author of *Works and Days* and *Theogony*.

Hippocrates (c. 460–c. 370 B.C.). Greek physician; traditionally regarded as the father of medicine. Author of *The Aphorisms*.

Holmes, Oliver Wendell, Jr. (1841–1935). Legal historian, philosopher and Supreme Court Justice. Author of *The Common Law* (1881).

Holmes, Oliver Wendell, Sr. (1809–1894). American physician, poet and humorist. Author of *Old Ironsides* (1830) and *The Autocrat of the Breakfast-Table* (1858).

Hoover, Herbert Clark (1874–1964). Thirty-first president of the United States (1929–33). Author of *American Individualism* (1922) and *Memoirs* (1951–52).

Howe, Edgar Watson (1853–1937). American journalist, novelist and essayist; nicknamed "The Sage of Potato Hill." Author of *The Story of a Country Town* (1883) and *Ventures in Common Sense* (1919).

Hubbard, Elbert Green (1856–1915). American editor, publisher and essayist. Author of *A Message to Garcia* (1899).

Hubbard, Frank McKinney "Kin" (1868–1930). American humorist. Author of *Abe Martin's Sayings and Sketches* (1915).

Hugo, Victor (1802–1885). French poet, playwright and novelist. Author of *The Hunchback of Notre Dame* (1831) and *Les Misérables* (1862).

Huxley, Aldous Leonard (1894–1963). English novelist, poet and essayist. Author of *Point Counter Point* (1928) and *Brave New World* (1932).

Huxley, Thomas Henry (1825–1895). English biologist and educator. Author of *Evolution and Ethics* (1893).

Ibsen, Henrik (1828–1906). Norwegian poet and playwright. Author of *A Doll's House* (1879), *An Enemy of the People* (1882) and *Hedda Gabler* (1890).

Imhoff, John (1923–). American industrial engineer.

Ingersoll, Robert G. (1833–1899). American lawyer, politician and orator. Author of *Why I Am an Agnostic* (1896).

Jefferson, Thomas (1743–1826). Third president of the United States (1801–09). Principal author of the *Declaration of Independence* (1776); author of *Notes on the State of Virginia* (1787).

Johnson, Samuel (1709–1784). English poet, essayist, critic, journalist, lexicographer and conversationalist. Author of the *Dictionary of the English Language* (1755) and *Lives of the Poets* (1779–81).

Jones, Thomas F., Dr. (1916–1981). American professor of engineering.

Jonson, Ben (c. 1572–1637). English, poet, playwright and critic. Author of *Volpone* (1605) and *The Alchemist* (1610).

Joubert, Joseph (1754–1824). French moralist. Author of *Pensées*.

Juvenal (Decimus Junius Juvenalis) (fl. 1st to 2nd century A.D.). Roman poet. Author of *Satires*.

Kelly, James (n.d./18th century).

Keyes, Francis Parkinson (1885–1970). American novelist. Author of *Queen Anne's Lace* (1930).

Kierkegaard, Søren (1813–1855). Danish religious philosopher. Author of *Either/Or* (1843) and *Fragments* (1844).

King, Martin Luther, Jr. (1929–1968). American clergyman, civil-rights leader and Nobel Prize winner (1964).

Kroc, Ray A. (1902–1984). American businessman; founder of McDonald's.

La Bruyère, Jean de (1645–1696). French writer and moralist. Author of *Characters* (1688).

La Fayette, Marie Madeleine de (1634–1693). French novelist.

La Fontaine, Jean de (1621–1695). French poet and fabulist.

Lao-tzu (c. 604–c. 531 B.C.). Chinese philosopher; founder of Taoism. Traditionally regarded as the author of *Tao-te-ching*.

Laplace, Pierre Simon, Marquis de (1749–1827). French mathematician, astronomer and physicist. Author of *Celestial Mechanics* (1799–1825).

Lardner, Ring (1885–1933). American humorist and short story writer. Author of *Gullible's Travels* (1917) and *How to Write Short Stories (With Samples)* (1924).

Lenclos, Ninon de (1620–1705). French beauty and *salon* wit.

La Rochefoucauld, François, Duc de (1613–1680). French writer and social reformer. Author of *Maxims* (1665).

Leonardo da Vinci (1452–1519). Italian painter, sculptor, architect and inventor. Author of *Notebooks*.

Lichtenberg, Georg Christoph (1742–1799). German physicist and satirist. Author of *Aphorisms* (1764–99).

Lincoln, Abraham (1809–1865). Sixteenth president of the United States (1861–65). Author of the *Emancipation Proclamation* (1863) and the *Gettysburg Address* (1863).

Lippmann, Walter (1889–1974). American journalist. Author of *The Good Society* (1937) and *Western Unity and the Common Market* (1962).

Locke, John (1632–1704). English empirical philosopher. Author of *An Essay Concerning Human Understanding* (1690).

Lois, George (1931–). American advertising executive. Author of *George Be Careful* (1972) and *The Art of Advertising: George Lois on Mass Communication* (1977).

Longfellow, Henry Wadsworth (1807–1882) American poet. Author of *Evangeline* (1847), *The Song of Hiawatha* (1855), and *Paul Revere's Ride* (1861).

Lowell, James Russell (1819–1891). American poet, critic and diplomat. Author of *A Fable for Critics* (1848) and *The Bigelow Papers* (1848; 2d series, 1867).

Lyly, John (c. 1554–1606). English prose stylist and playwright. Author of *Euphues or the Anatomy of Wit* (1578) and *Euphues and His England* (1580).

MacLaine, Shirley (1934–). American actress.

Marchant, Henry (1704–1796). American statesman.

Marcus Aurelius (121–180). Emperor of Rome and Stoic philosopher. Author of *Meditations*.

Martial (Marcus Valerius Martialis) (c. 40–c. 104). Roman epigrammatic poet.

McLuhan, Marshall Herbert (1911–1980). Canadian communications specialist and educator. Author of *The Mechanical Bride: Folklore of Industrial Man* (1951) and *Understanding Media: The Extensions of Man* (1964).

Meir, Golda (1898–1978). Prime minister of Israel (1969–74).

Mill, John Stuart (1806–1873). English Utilitarian philosopher and political economist. Author of *A System of Logic* (1843), *Principles of Political Economy* (1848) and *Autobiography* (1873).

Molière (Jean Baptiste Poquelin) (1622–1673). French dramatist. Author of *Tartuffe* (1664) and *Le Misanthrope* (1666).

Montesquieu, Charles de Secondat, Baron de (1689–1755). French political philosopher. Author of *Persian Letters* (1721) and *The Spirit of Laws* (1748).

Moore, George (1852–1933). Irish novelist and man of letters. Author of *Esther Waters* (1894).

Nietzsche, Friedrich Wilhelm (1844–1900). German philosopher. Author of *The Birth of Tragedy* (1872) and *Beyond Good and Evil* (1886).

Nightingale, Florence (1820–1910). English nurse, hospital reformer and philanthropist.

Orwell, George (Eric Arthur Blair) (1903–1950). English novelist, essayist and critic. Author of *Animal Farm* (1946) and *Nineteen Eighty-four* (1949).

Osler, Sir William (1849–1919). English physician. Author of *The Principles and Practice of Medicine* (1892).

Paine, Thomas (1737–1809). American political journalist. Author of *Common Sense* (1776), *The Rights of Man* (1791–92) and *The Age of Reason* (1794–95).

Pankhurst, Christabel (1880–1958). English suffragette.

Parkinson, Cyril Northcote (1909–). American historian and playwright. Author of *Parkinson's Law* (1957).

Pascal, Blaise (1623–1662). French scientist and religious philosopher. Author of *Pensées* (1670).

Patton, George S. (1885–1945). American general. Author of *War as I Knew It* (1947).

Pavlov, Ivan Petrovich (1849–1936). Russian physiologist, psychologist and Nobel Prize winner (1904). Author of *Conditioned Reflexes* (1927).

Pepys, Samuel (1633–1703). English man of letters, naval administrator and diarist.

Pericles (c. 495–429 B.C.). Athenian statesman, military commander and orator.

Perkins, Francis (1882–1965). American labor activist and U.S. Secretary of Labor (1933–45).

Petronius, Gaius (d. c. 66 A.D.). Roman consul. Reputed author of *Satyricon*.

Phillips, Wendell (1811–1884). American abolitionist and orator.

Piozzi, Hester Lynch Thrale (1741–1821). English writer. Author of *Anecdotes of the Late Samuel Johnson* (1786).

Pittacus (c. 650–c. 570 B.C.). Mytilenean statesman, known as one of the Seven Wise Men of Greece.

Plato (c. 427–347 B.C.). Greek philosopher. Author of the *Symposium* and the *Republic*.

Plutarch (c. 46–c. 120 A.D.). Greek essayist and biographer. Author of *The Parallel Lives*.

Poincaré, Jules Henri (1854–1912). French mathematician, astronomer and philosopher of science. Author of *Science and Hypothesis* (1905).

Post, Emily (1873–1960). American authority on manners. Author of *Etiquette* (1922).

Pound, Roscoe (1870–1964). American jurist and botanist. Author of *The Spirit of the Common Law* (1921).

Publilius Syrus (1st century B.C.). Latin writer of mimes. Author of *Sententiae*.

Pulitzer, Joseph (1847–1911). American newspaper editor and publisher. Established the Pulitzer Prizes.

Quillen, Robert (1887–1948). American writer. Author of *The Path Warton Found* (1924).

Rockefeller, John D. (1839–1937). American industrialist, philanthropist and founder of the Standard Oil Company.

Roosevelt, Eleanor (1884–1962). Wife of U.S. President Franklin Delano Roosevelt; lecturer, writer and humanitarian.

Roosevelt, Theodore (1858–1919). Twenty-sixth president of the United States (1901–9) and writer. Author of *The New Nationalism* (1910) and *Progressive Principles* (1913).

Roux, Joseph (1834–1905). French priest and writer. Author of *Meditations of a Parish Priest* (1886).

Russell, Bertrand Arthur William (1872–1970). English philosopher, mathematician and social reformer. Author of (with A.N. Whitehead) *Principia Mathematica* (1910–13) and *Marriage and Morals* (1929).

Sagan, Françoise (1935–). French novelist. Author of *Bonjour Tristesse* (1954).

Sanger, Margaret (1883–1966). American leader of the birth-control movement. Author of *Happiness in Marriage* (1926).

Santayana, George (1863–1952). American philosopher, poet and novelist. Author of *The Life of Reason* (1905–06) and *The Last Puritan* (1935).

Schiller, Friedrich von (1759–1805). German dramatist, poet and literary theorist. Author of *Maria Stuart* (1800) and *Wilhelm Tell* (1804).

Selfridge, H. Gordon (1857–1947). American-British founder of Selfridge's department store.

Seneca, Lucius Annaeus (c. 4 B.C.–65 A.D.). Roman statesman and philosopher. Author of *Epistolae morales* and *Dialogi*.

Shakespeare, William (1564–1616). English dramatist and poet. Author of *A Midsummer Night's Dream* (1600), *Hamlet* (1603) and *King Lear* (1608).

Shanahan, Eileen (1924–) American journalist.

Shaw, George Bernard (1856–1950). British playwright and Nobel Prize winner (1925). Author of *Man and Superman* (1905), *Major Barbara* (1905), *Pygmalion* (1913) and *Saint Joan* (1923).

Sloan, Alfred P., Jr. (1875–1966). American industrialist and former chairman of the board of the General Motors Corporation. Author of *My Years with General Motors* (1964).

Smiles, Samuel (1812–1904). Scottish author of *Self-Help* (1859), *Character* (1871), *Thrift* (1875) and *Duty* (1880).

Smith, Alexander (1830–1867). Scottish poet and essayist. Author of *Dreamthorp* (1863).

Smith, Logan Pearsall (1865–1946). American-British scholar and man of letters. Author of *The English Language* (1912), *All Trivia* (1933) and *On Reading Shakespeare* (1933).

Socrates (c. 470–399 B.C.). Greek philosopher.

Sophocles (c. 496–406 B.C.). Greek tragedian. Author of *Oedipus Rex*, *Philoctetes*, *Antigone* and *Electra*.

Staël, Germaine de (1766–1817). French-Swiss woman of letters. Author of *Corinne* (1807) and *De l'Allemagne* (1810).

Steffens, Lincoln (1866–1936). American journalist and muckraker. Author of *The Shame of the Cities* (1904) and *Lincoln Steffens Speaking* (1936).

Stein, Gertrude (1874–1946). American expatriate writer. Author of *Three Lives* (1909), *The Making of Americans* (1925) and *The Autobiography of Alice B. Toklas* (1933).

Stevenson, Adlai Ewing (1900–1965). American statesman. Author of *Friends and Enemies* (1959) and *Putting First Things First* (1960).

Stevenson, Robert Louis (1850–1894). Scottish novelist, poet and essayist. Author of *Treasure Island* (1883), *The Strange Case of Dr. Jekyll and Mr. Hyde* (1886) and *Kidnapped* (1886).

Tacitus, Cornelius (c. 55–c. 117 A.D.). Roman historian. Author of *Histories* and the *Annals*.

Thatcher, Margaret (1925–). Prime minister of Britain (1979–1990).

Thomas à Kempis (1379–1471). German monk. Author of *The Imitation of Christ* (c. 1427).

Thoreau, Henry David (1817–1862). American essayist, poet, and philosopher. Author of *Walden* (1854) and "Civil Disobedience" (1849).

Thucydides (c. 471–c. 400 B.C.). Greek historian. Author of *History of the Peloponnesian War*.

Titchener, Edward Bradford (1867–1927). American psychologist. Author of *Experimental Psychology* (1901–05).

Truman, Harry S. (1884–1972). Thirty-third president of the United States (1945–53). Architect of the Truman Doctrine and the Marshall Plan.

Truth, Sojourner (1797–1883). American feminist and abolitionist.

Tseng-tzu (5th century B.C.). Disciple of Confucius. Author of *The Great Learning*.

Twain, Mark (Samuel Langhorne Clemens) (1835–1910). American humorist, novelist, newspaperman and lecturer. Author of *The Adventures of Tom Sawyer* (1876) and *The Adventures of Huckleberry Finn* (1884).

Vauvenargues, Luc de Clapiers, Marquis de (1715–1747). French moralist and essayist.

Veblen, Thorstein (1857–1929). American economist and social scientist. Author of *The Theory of the Leisure Class* (1899) and *The Theory of Business Enterprise* (1904).

Voltaire (François Marie Arouet de) (1694–1778). French philosopher and man of letters. Author of *Candide* (1759) and *Philosophical Dictionary* (1764).

Vorster, John (1915–). Prime minister of the Republic of South Africa (1966–78).

Wallace, Lewis (1827–1905). American soldier, lawyer, diplomat and novelist. Author of *The Fair God* (1873) and *Ben Hur* (1880).

Webb, Beatrice Potter (1858–1943). English socialist and economist. Author of *The Cooperative Movement in Great Britain* (1891).

Webb, Mary (1881–1927). English novelist. Author of *Precious Bane* (1924).

Wilde, Oscar (1854–1900). Irish wit, poet, dramatist, novelist and essayist. Author of *The Picture of Dorian Gray* (1891), *Lady Windemere's Fan* (1892) and *The Importance of Being Ernest* (1895).

Woolf, Virginia (1882–1941). English novelist and essayist. Author of *The Common Reader* (1925), *To the Lighthouse* (1927) and *A Room of One's Own* (1929).

Wright, Frank Lloyd (1869–1959). American architect and writer. Author of *Genius and the Mobocracy* (1949) and *The Future of Architecture* (1953).

My Personal Notes

My Favorite Quotes